Contents

Why Do Things Move?

When things begin to move or change direction, it means that a force has been used. A force pulls or pushes an object.

Why Things Move

WELDON OWEN PTY LTD

Publisher: Sheena Coupe
Senior Designer: Kylie Mulquin
Editorial Coordinators: Sarah Anderson,
Tracey Gibson
Production Manager: Helen Creeke
Production Assistant: Kylie Lawson

Project Editor: Ariana Klepac
Designer: Patricia Ansell
Text: Jan Stradling

05 04 03
10 9 8 7 6 5 4 3 2

Published in the United States by
Wright Group/McGraw-Hill
19201 120th Avenue NE, Suite 100
Bothell, WA 98011
www.WrightGroup.com

Printed in Singapore
ISBN: 0-7699-1222-2
ISBN: 0-7699-1466-7 (6-pack)

CREDITS AND ACKNOWLEDGMENTS

PICTURE AND ILLUSTRATION CREDITS
[t=top, b=bottom, l=left, r=right, c=center]
Ad-Libitum 3tr, 3br, 4-5bl, 5tr, 9tl, 12l, 14c, 16c, 24bc (S. Bowey). **Colin Brown/illustration** 22t, 23r. **Tom Connell/Wildlife Art Ltd.** 10b, 11b. **Corel Corporation** 5br, 8bc, banding. **Christer Eriksson** 19tr, 19bl. **Ray Grinaway** 9cr. **David Kirshner** 19tl. **Frank Knight** 9bc. **Alex Lavroff** 12cr. **Nature Focus** 15bc (C. Bento). **Sandra Pond/Wildlife Art Ltd.** 11t. **Photodisc** 1c, 12bc, 15tr. **PhotoEssentials** 7c. **Oliver Rennert** 19br. **John Richards** 13c. **Claudia Saraceni** 9bl. **Stephen Seymour/Bernard Thornton Artists UK** 23l. **Shortland Publications** 5tl, 6bl, 6tr (Mary Foley). **Rod Westblade** 18c. **Ann Winterbotham** 9tr.

Weldon Owen would like to thank the following people for their assistance in the production of this book: Peta Gorman, Michael Hann, Marney Richardson.

Pushes and pulls help us carry out many actions. Pushes and pulls help us get jobs done.

A force makes the ball move when the boy kicks it.

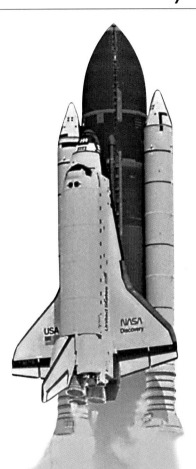

What force
makes the
space shuttle
lift off?

Gravity

When we jump up we always come down again. This is because of a force called gravity. Gravity pulls things back toward Earth.

Gravity pulls the parachute down to Earth.

Gravity affects everybody
and everything in the world.

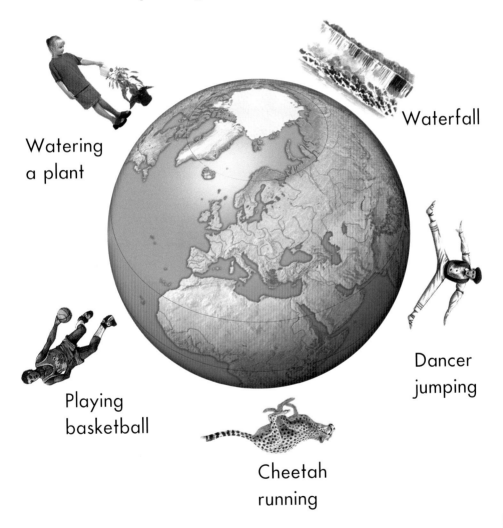

Waterfall

Watering
a plant

Playing
basketball

Dancer
jumping

Cheetah
running

Rockets have to be very powerful to pull away from the Earth's gravity. The Moon's gravity is weaker than the Earth's. This is why things feel much lighter on the Moon.

A ball goes farther on the Moon.

Did You Know?

A black hole in space
has very strong gravity.
It pulls in anything near it.
Once trapped, not even light can escape.

Gravity holds
satellites
on their path
circling
the Earth.

Friction

Friction is a force that happens when two surfaces rub together. Rough surfaces rubbing against one another create more friction. Friction slows things down.

The dolphin is smooth. It moves quickly through water.

Rubber soles grip the ground.

Skis slide over snow.

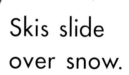

The tread
on tires helps
keep the bikes
from skidding.

Magnets

Magnets are often made
from a metal called iron.
Magnets pull or push
other objects with
a magnetic force.
They do this without
touching them.

Magnets can
attract more
than one object
at a time.

Pigeons use the Earth's magnetism to find their way home.

Lodestone is a rock that is magnetic.

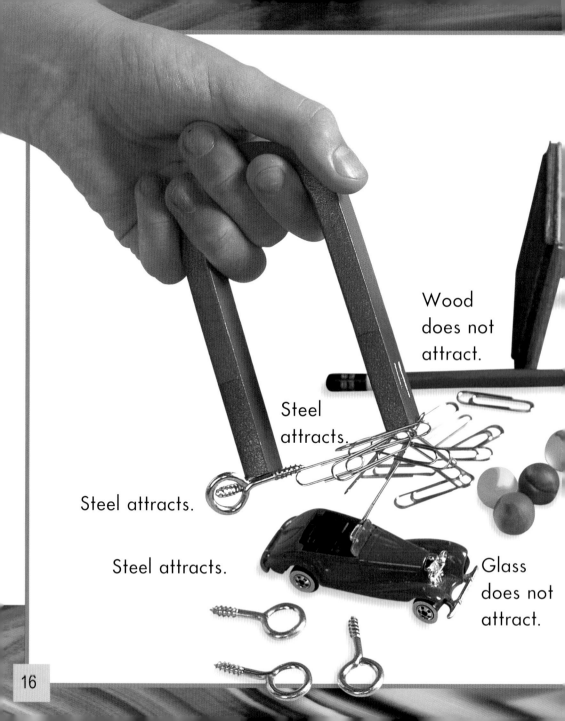

Wood does not attract.

Steel attracts.

Steel attracts.

Steel attracts.

Glass does not attract.

Magnets attract objects made of iron and steel. If the object does not contain iron or steel, it will not move toward the magnet.

Plastic does not attract.

Rubber does not attract.

The magnet does not attract the stamp, the pencil, the eraser, or the marbles.

Pole to Pole

All magnets have two ends called poles. One end is the north pole and the other is the south pole.

Opposite poles attract each other.

The same poles repel each other.

The Earth is a magnet.
It has two poles.

The Arctic (North Pole)

Polar bears

The Antarctic (South Pole)

Adelie penguins

Magnetic Fields

There is an invisible magnetic field around every magnet. You can see the shape of the field by putting iron filings on top of a piece of paper, and putting two magnets underneath.

Auroras

The Earth's magnetic field causes colored lights, called auroras, to shine in the sky near the poles.

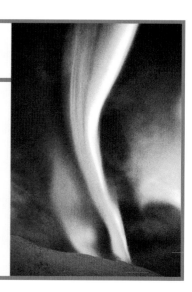

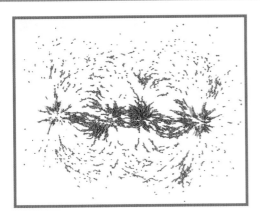 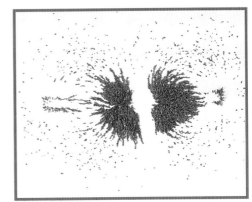

The iron filing pattern shows that magnetic fields of opposite poles attract each other.

The iron filing pattern shows that magnetic fields of the same poles repel each other.

The Earth's magnetic field makes a compass point north/south.

21

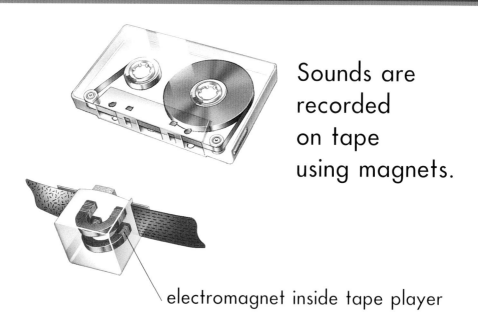

Sounds are
recorded
on tape
using magnets.

electromagnet inside tape player

Electromagnets

An electromagnet uses electricity
to make magnetic fields
and can be switched on and off.
We use electromagnets in many
different machines.

Maglev Train

This train travels on a cushion of magnetic fields. The train does not touch the tracks.

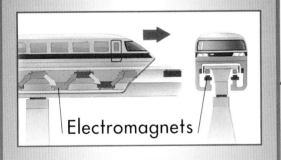
Electromagnets

There are electromagnets in this tape player.

Index